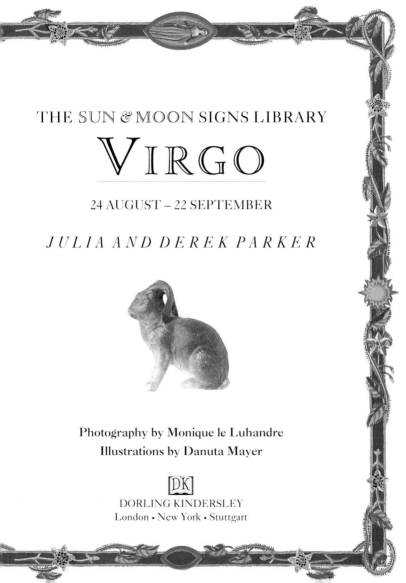

THE SUN & MOON SIGNS LIBRARY

VIRGO

24 AUGUST – 22 SEPTEMBER

JULIA AND DEREK PARKER

Photography by Monique le Luhandre
Illustrations by Danuta Mayer

[DK]
DORLING KINDERSLEY
London • New York • Stuttgart

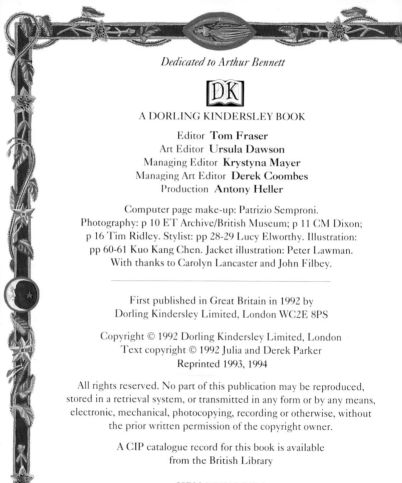

Dedicated to Arthur Bennett

DK

A DORLING KINDERSLEY BOOK

Editor **Tom Fraser**
Art Editor **Ursula Dawson**
Managing Editor **Krystyna Mayer**
Managing Art Editor **Derek Coombes**
Production **Antony Heller**

Computer page make-up: Patrizio Semproni.
Photography: p 10 ET Archive/British Museum; p 11 CM Dixon;
p 16 Tim Ridley. Stylist: pp 28-29 Lucy Elworthy. Illustration:
pp 60-61 Kuo Kang Chen. Jacket illustration: Peter Lawman.
With thanks to Carolyn Lancaster and John Filbey.

First published in Great Britain in 1992 by
Dorling Kindersley Limited, London WC2E 8PS

A CIP catalogue record for this book is available
from the British Library

ISBN 0-86318-849-4

Reproduced by GRB Editrice, Verona, Italy
Printed and bound in Hong Kong by Imago

CONTENTS

INTRODUCING
VIRGO

VIRGO, THE SIGN OF THE VIRGIN, IS THE SIXTH SIGN OF THE
ZODIAC. BECAUSE IT IS RULED BY THE PLANET
MERCURY, VIRGOANS OFTEN TEND TO BE EXCELLENT, IF
SOMETIMES HYPERCRITICAL, COMMUNICATORS.

Modesty is a common Virgoan trait, and Virgoans often express themselves in a self-effacing manner. You must be careful not to underestimate your capabilities, and should constantly try to build up your self-confidence. While Virgoans achieve inner satisfaction by helping and serving others, this can lead to you being imposed upon.

Virgoans tend to be practical and hardworking, but the influence of the planet Mercury can make you restless, and you may tend to do too much. You should plan your days well in advance, so that there is time for relaxation. This will also help counter stress, to which you are prone.

Traditional groupings

As you read through this book you will come across references to the elements and the qualities, and to positive and negative, or masculine and feminine signs.

The first of these groupings, that of the elements, comprises fire, earth, air, and water signs. The second, that of the qualities, divides the Zodiac into cardinal, fixed, and mutable signs. The final grouping is made up of positive and negative, or masculine and feminine signs. Each Zodiac sign is associated with a combination of components from these groupings, all of which contribute different characteristics to it.

Virgoan characteristics

Virgo is a sign of the earth element, and contact with the earth is often of importance to Virgoans. Many of them are superb gardeners.

Virgo is also a sign of the mutable quality, which bestows a flexible mind and a good intellect. Being a negative, feminine sign its subjects tend to be introverts. According to tradition, navy blue, dark brown, and green are Virgoan colours.

ARIES PISCES AQUARIUS CAPRICORN SAGITTARIUS SCORPIO LIBRA VIRGO LEO CANCER GEMINI TAURUS

The Zodiac Wheel

The relationship between each Zodiac sign and the traditional astrological groupings is made clear within the Zodiac wheel. As you read through this book you will also discover references to polar, or opposite signs, and these, too, can be easily worked out by referring to the wheel.

CARDINAL

MASCULINE MUTABLE

FEMININE FIXED

FIRE

EARTH

AIR

WATER

VIRGO
MYTHS & LEGENDS

THE ZODIAC, WHICH IS SAID TO HAVE ORIGINATED IN BABYLON
POSSIBLY AS LONG AS 2,500 YEARS AGO, IS A CIRCLE
OF CONSTELLATIONS THROUGH WHICH THE SUN MOVES
DURING THE COURSE OF A YEAR.

The sign Virgo is thought to have been named in Ancient Babylon, or perhaps Sumeria, and the original Virgin that represents the sign is considered to have been Nidaba or Shala, a grain goddess. In one ancient tablet she is described as having "a star on her head and a whip in her right hand, the thong of which stretches out over the tail of Leo". (Similarly, in an Ancient Egyptian zodiac, at Esna, Virgo is shown holding Leo by the tail.) As time passed, however, the conception of a matronly goddess slowly evolved. She was gradually rendered as more youthful, and she is perceived in modern representations as being a beautiful young maiden.

Elizabeth I (1533-1603)
*Those who surrounded this
English queen kindly compared
her to the "starry maiden".*

In the first century B.C., the famous Roman writer, Marcus Manilius, set out an early account of astrological mythology in his *Astronomica*. He mentions two myths in relation to Virgo. In the first myth he claims that the original virgin was a young girl named Erigone, the daughter of Icarius, king of Attica and the first mortal maker of wine. Unfortunately, his gift led to Icarius's downfall: he unwisely gave some liquor to a party of shepherds, who then drunkenly murdered him. His faithful dog, Maera, took Erigone by the hem of her gown and led her to his grave, above which she hanged herself in

Ancient Map of the Heavens
This early astrological chart, "Atlas Coelistis Hemisphaerium Stellatum Boreale", dates from 1660. On it can be seen representations of each of the constellations.

grief. Zeus, king of the gods, set Maera in the skies as the Dog-star, and Erigone as Virgo.

The starry maiden

As an alternative figure for Virgo, Manilius offers Astraea, the "starry maiden", who has long been identified with Justice, and was the last of the gods to leave the Earth. Astraea lived among men in the Golden Age, but fled to heaven when mankind grew to unwisdom. The English queen Elizabeth I, also known as the Virgin Queen, was often referred to as Astraea by the sycophants who surrounded her.

It is important to remember that the earliest associations of Virgo had far more to do with beauty and kindness than with virginity and coldness. Indeed, the modern emphasis on the cool frigidity of the sign is quite ridiculous.

VIRGO
SYMBOLISM

CERTAIN HERBS, SPICES, FLOWERS, TREES, GEMS, METALS, AND
ANIMALS HAVE LONG BEEN ASSOCIATED WITH PARTICULAR
ZODIAC SIGNS. SOME ASSOCIATIONS ARE SIMPLY FUN, WHILE
OTHERS CAN BE USEFUL, FOR INSTANCE IN MEDICINE.

BLUE
BUTTERFLY

Flowers
*Red, pink, bright yellow, and bright blue
flowers, particularly the cornflower,
are associated with Virgo.*

CORNFLOWER

Trees
Nut-bearing trees are associated with the planet Mercury, which rules Virgo.

OAK

BEECH

Spices
No spice is traditionally associated with Virgo, but cinnamon and cardamom are sometimes mentioned.

CARDAMOM

CINNAMON

Herbs
Any herb that has a red or a pink flower comes under the rulership of Virgo.

LEMON BALM

VIRGO SYMBOLISM

Gem

The Virgoan stone is sardonyx, which is composed of onyx, a kind of quartz, layered with sard, the yellow colour of which no doubt led to the association.

SARD SEALS

Metal

As with Gemini, mercury is a Virgoan metal. So is nickel, with its silvery white, lustrous quality.

EBONY MOUSE

NICKEL

CERAMIC RABBIT

PORCELAIN
HARE

TOY METAL RABBIT

Animals

*Small cats and most domestic pets
come under the dominion of
Virgo. All female animals are,
however, to some extent
ruled by Virgo.*

CERAMIC CONTAINER
DECORATED WITH RABBITS

VIRGO
PROFILE

QUICK, SLIGHTLY JERKY MOVEMENTS OF THE HEAD AND HANDS, A
VERY NEAT IMAGE, AND AN OVERALL AIR OF ACTIVITY ARE
TYPICAL OF THIS ZODIAC GROUP. AS A VIRGOAN, YOU ARE ALWAYS
LIKELY TO BE "ON THE GO"

Some Virgoans have a tendency to stoop. If this is the case with you, make every effort to ensure that you do not become round-shouldered. As a Virgoan, you probably keep your feet close together, and your hands clasped in front of you. While you release your hands frequently in order to gesticulate, they are usually quickly and firmly clasped again. When kept waiting, you strum your fingers impatiently. Virgoans usually have no time to waste, after all.

The Virgoan face

Virgoans often possess very quizzical expressions. You rarely miss a thing.

The body
Virgoans tend to have rather elongated bodies and limbs; their bone structures are also usually very

prominent. However, because they can be very well-proportioned people, this can make them look extremely photogenic, as opposed to awkward.

The face
Your hair is likely to be well cut and cared for. In the case of many Virgoans it will also appear sleek, and people of either sex may have "widow's peaks". Virgoan eyes are usually very clear, alert, and bright, and tend to dart from side to side with curiosity – Virgoans can sometimes be a little too curious. Your nose might be rather sharp, as could your chin, and your mouth is probably quite small. You may purse your lips when you are worried. Many Virgoans have an

The Virgoan stance

Many Virgoans tend to stand with both of their feet placed close together, and their hands clasped in front of them.

xtremely quizzical appearance. In
act, you might give the impression of
ever missing a single thing.

tyle

ou are likely to favour navy blue and
ather dark colours, or small floral
atterns that are sometimes quite
rightly coloured. The neat Virgoan
usinessman often wears a colourful
loral tie, and his white collars and
uffs will stay pristine all day. Virgoan
omen often choose a Victorian look,
nd may dress in country styles, using
atural fabrics.

The majority of Virgoans enjoy
earching for high-quality clothes that
ave a long life ahead of them, as
pposed to fashion items that become
edundant after being worn only once.

Virgoans usually like wearing high-
uality leather gloves, and beautifully
ade belts. However, a hat is
omething that you are likely to wear
nly for practical reasons. Overall,
our image is likely to reflect Virgoan
nodesty, and to be extraordinarily
eat, but it has a very special, alluring
harm all of its own.

In general

Your bright personality is probably
reflected in the quick movements
that you make, and through a fast,
rather bouncy walk. You sometimes
tend to be rather fussy, and may be
prone to flicking imaginary bits of lint
from your clothes or playing with a
string of beads. Due to slight
nervousness, you may have a
tendency to blink a lot.

VIRGO
PERSONALITY

VIRGOANS ARE THE WORKERS OF THE ZODIAC, AND ALWAYS ENJOY
WORKING FOR OTHER PEOPLE IN ONE WAY OR ANOTHER.
WHILE PRACTICAL, WITH PLENTY OF COMMON SENSE, THEY ARE
NOT VERY GOOD ORGANIZERS.

All Virgoans like to keep busy. In fact, many never seem to stop, and find it hard to even sit and listen to a conversation.

At work
The need to serve, or to work for other people, is a very important part of the Virgoan psychological motivation. As a direct result of this, many Sun sign Virgoans make excellent personal assistants, or they may find themselves positions in which they are either helping or serving other people.

You will like to know what you have to do and when you have to do it by. It may be that your tendency to be a poor organizer stems from a certain lack of self-confidence. This, in turn, is frequently outwardly expressed through a delightful, if often over-played, modesty. You will feel, and perhaps say, that you cannot do something, and then go on to give

many reasons why, and name a lot of other people who, in your opinion, could do it better. It is at times like this that friends and family are in a position to help Virgoans the most. Self-effacement has charm, but it can occasionally go too far.

Your attitudes
The influence of Virgo's ruling planet, Mercury, is interesting. It is liable to make you an exceptionally good communicator, and usually pretty talkative. You are excellent at expressing your opinions, and do not need much encouragement to do so.

Mercury's influence is liable to make you very critical, and could give you the ability to analyze problems in detail. As a result, Virgoans are often able to carve out successful careers for themselves in the media. However, if you feel a need to be critical in the context of personal relationships, you would be wise to exercise a little

Mercury rules Virgo

Mercury, the messenger god, represents the ruling planet of Virgo.
The influence of Mercury stimulates the mind, but it can also
make its subjects critical, nervous, and tense.

restraint. No one will appreciate a person who is frequently prone to nagging and criticizing their partners and friends. You do not want to obtain a reputation for being too fussy.

The overall picture

Virgoans are, for all of the reasons that have been mentioned, exceptionally prone to worry. If, however, you put yourself into a position whereby you approach whatever it is that happens to be bothering you using your natural logic and analytical acumen, you are sure to come up with some really practical answers. Making comprehensive lists of the pros and cons of a difficult situation could help you to assess and analyze it in the necessary detail.

VIRGO
ASPIRATIONS

YOU COULD EASILY BE AN EXCELLENT SECRETARY OR PERSONAL
ASSISTANT, BUT REMEMBER THAT YOU ARE CAPABLE OF
MORE THAN MERE SUBSERVIENCE. TO SATISFY YOUR NEED FOR
SECURITY, YOU SHOULD MAKE YOURSELF INDISPENSABLE.

Agriculture
*Because earth is the
Virgoan element, working
in agriculture or
horticulture may come
naturally to you.*

MODEL TRACTOR

Librarianship
*A career that combines serving the
public and working with books
could prove to be very satisfying.
Similarly, you may find bookshop
work appealing.*

INK PAD,
DATE STAMP,
AND BOOKS

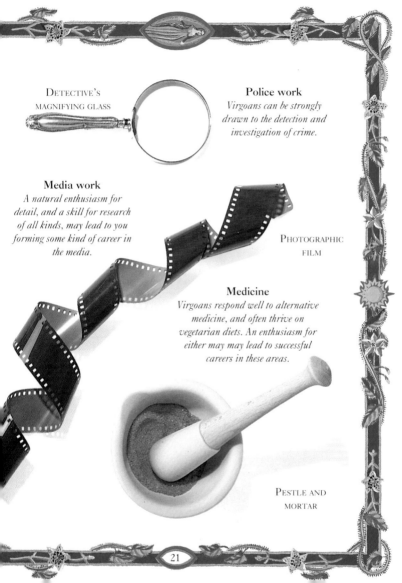

Detective's
magnifying glass

Police work
*Virgoans can be strongly
drawn to the detection and
investigation of crime.*

Media work
*A natural enthusiasm for
detail, and a skill for research
of all kinds, may lead to you
forming some kind of career in
the media.*

Photographic
film

Medicine
*Virgoans respond well to alternative
medicine, and often thrive on
vegetarian diets. An enthusiasm for
either may may lead to successful
careers in these areas.*

Pestle and
mortar

HEALTH

A STEADY CONSUMPTION OF NERVOUS AND PHYSICAL ENERGY IS
VITAL TO KEEP THE VIRGOAN SYSTEM IN GOOD ORDER.
FRUSTRATION AND WORRY WILL LEAD TO PHYSICAL PROBLEMS,
AND PSYCHOLOGICAL AND MENTAL STAGNATION.

The high level of nervous energy that most Virgoans have needs to be worked off through really satisfying work. The discipline of a relaxation technique, like yoga or meditation, can also sometimes help to calm Virgoans and get their nervous energy under control.

Your diet
Virgoans benefit from a diet that is high in fibre. It is worth noting that, before vegetarianism was fashionable, Virgoans were most inclined to it, as well as to homeopathy and complementary medical techniques.

You may benefit from the cell salt Kali sulphicurum (Kali. Sulph.), which is said to help prevent bronchitis.

Taking care
The Virgoan body area is the stomach. Because of this many Virgoans find themselves suffering from stomach complaints when they are forced to bear strain or nervous tension. The whole nervous system is actually related to Virgo, so the fact that it is very easily upset by external influences is hardly surprising. If Virgoans become tense, there is also a good chance that they might end up succumbing to migraines.

Hazelnuts
As with Gemini, most nuts are traditionally considered to be Virgoan foodstuffs.

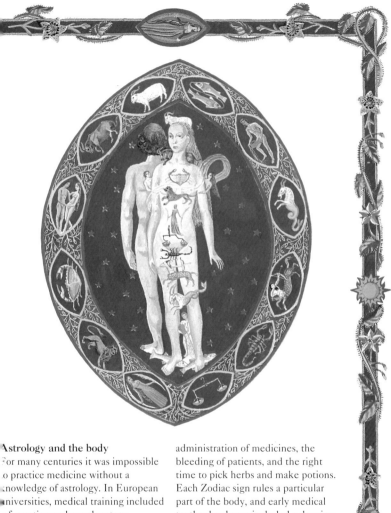

Astrology and the body

For many centuries it was impossible to practice medicine without a knowledge of astrology. In European universities, medical training included information on how planetary positions would affect the administration of medicines, the bleeding of patients, and the right time to pick herbs and make potions. Each Zodiac sign rules a particular part of the body, and early medical textbooks always included a drawing that illustrated the point.

VIRGO AT
LEISURE

EACH OF THE SUN SIGNS TRADITIONALLY SUGGESTS SPARE-TIME
ACTIVITIES, HOBBIES, AND HOLIDAY DESTINATIONS.
ALTHOUGH THESE ARE ONLY SUGGESTIONS, THEY OFTEN WORK
OUT WELL, AND ARE WORTH TESTING.

POSTAGE STAMPS

Sports
*Outdoor sports of all
kinds, like cycling or
golf, will probably
appeal to you.*

CIGARETTE CARDS
SHOWING CYCLING

Travel
*As a Virgoan, you will like
visiting mountainous places.
A trip to Syria, Brazil,
Iraq, the West Indies, or
Czechoslovakia may
also appeal to you.*

Gardening
*Virgo is an earth sign, and
many Virgoans
specialize in
growing
vegetables or
small, brightly
coloured
flowers.*

GARDENING
GLOVES AND
SECATEURS

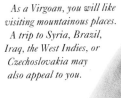

Pottery

You may obtain pleasure from working with natural materials, for example clay or wool.

POTTER'S
TOOLS

BOOKS AND
READING GLASSES

Reading

Virgoans often like to read biographies and critical essays. Some may enjoy family sagas.

Knitting

Homecrafts that require meticulous attention to detail, such as knitting, crochet work, intricate sewing, and tailoring, are often popular with Virgoans.

WOOL AND
KNITTING NEEDLES

VIRGO IN
LOVE

MODESTY AND SHYNESS, PERFECTIONISM AND A CRITICAL EYE, ARE
ALL CHARACTERISTIC OF THE VERY INDIVIDUAL VIRGOAN
ATTITUDE TO LOVE. VIRGOANS WILL PONDER LONG AND HARD
BEFORE COMMITTING THEMSELVES TO SOMEONE.

Having such inquiring minds, as well as a great deal of modesty and a certain apprehensive shyness, tends to make loving rather tricky for many people of this Sun sign group. Their reactions will frequently be to question their feelings, or to try and figure out why someone finds them attractive.

The celebrated Virgoan modesty is, in fact, often a most attractive feature. If a prospective partner proceeds slowly and with care, and develops a good degree of friendship and intellectual rapport with you, it is probable that a rewarding bond of affection, love, and sexual fulfilment will develop. You must, however, also play a part in a relationship. Most importantly, you should not look for excuses to criticize your partner.

As a lover
In extreme cases, some Virgoans can develop a very clinical attitude to sex. They may even consider it to be "dirty" in some way. If this is the case, professional counselling should be sought. On a more positive note, because Virgoans are likely to have inquiring minds, many are extremely curious about sex from a very early age and could indulge in considerable

experimentation in this sphere. The emotions of Virgo are not normally highly charged, and while Virgoans are generally ...rbally skilful and charming, they ...ay not always express their feelings ...wards their partners in a deeply ...ssionate way.

...ypes of Virgoan lover

...any Virgoans make really tender ...d caring partners. They can, ...wever, sometimes create a ...austrophobic atmosphere within a ...lationship. Other Virgoans have ...fine sense of drama, and ...splay a warm, fiery ...ssion towards their ...vers. A third type will ...ree with all that has ...en said about Virgo in ...ve: if they can increase ...eir self-confidence ...d relax, they will

enjoy rewarding relationships. Some Virgoans have a surprisingly relaxed attitude to love and this sphere of their lives is coloured by a powerful romantic streak. Their only problem is likely to be an unfortunate tendency to rush into a relationship because they feel incomplete without a partner. A final group consists of those Virgoans who have strong emotional and sexual feelings. Generally speaking they are very demanding of their partners.

VIRGO AT
HOME

NEATNESS AND PERHAPS AUSTERITY CAN MAKE THE TYPICAL
VIRGOAN HOME A LITTLE TOO CLINICAL FOR COMFORT.
ENDEARINGLY, HOWEVER, A CLUTTER OF SMALL ORNAMENTS
CAN HUMANIZE IT. THERE WILL BE PLENTY OF PLANTS.

The typical Virgoan home is pretty and neat. The colours are often very cheerful, and the rooms full of detail and clutter, as a result of your diverse and plentiful interests.

If you were able to live in the ideal environment of your choice, you would probably choose a home in the country. However, since city careers are common among Virgoans, unless you feel able to face long, and often tiring, hours spent commuting you may have to make do with a home in town.

It would probably be wise for you to look at a few properties located near parks or some other form of open space whenever you are deciding where to live.

Furniture

Virgoans are usually very attracted to natural materials, so wood, particularly wood that has been treated so that its richness and natural beauty show to full advantage, is favoured. This rich effect is usually enhanced by either wool or linen covers, since showy brocades or silks, and lavish or elaborate furniture, are not to the Virgoan taste. The Virgoan home

Potted plants
A selection of fascinating plants is likely to be very much in evidence in a typically Virgoan home.

sometimes has a rather ethnic look to it, and because Virgoans are practical people, durability is also very important.

You will find space in your living room for a writing desk or some kind of work table if you do not have a studio or workshop in which to relax and practice your favourite hobbies.

Soft furnishings

Checks and spots, and above all small floral patterns, are especially popular with Virgoans. It is very common to discover chintzes with a tiny flower or leaf design in either the kitchen or the living room, and the impression given is of neatness combined with a certain prettiness. This can occasionally translate into over-fussiness. The cushions in a Virgoan home can sometimes be rather hard, since most Virgoans are not that keen on really relaxing. They do not always list comfort very high among their priorities.

Decorative objects

On the whole, Virgoans tend to like tiny objects and rather unusual curios, such as miniature vases, small silver boxes, and tiny, neatly framed pictures of the family. Your choice of paintings will usually be taken from schools that work in great detail. Dutch interior paintings, particularly domestic scenes, often enhance Virgoan walls. Tidiness and neatness are qualities attributed to Virgoans and, on the surface, this is true. Chaos is normally reserved for cupboards, where it cannot be seen. A sunny corner in your home, such as a windowsill, usually contains plants that have spectacular foliage as well as flowers.

Dressmaker's dummy
Virgoans take great pride in their hobbies, and evidence of them (in this case sewing), is often visible in their homes.

THE
MOON
AND
YOU

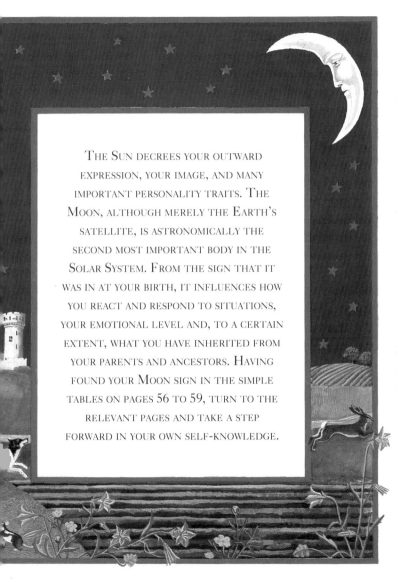

THE SUN DECREES YOUR OUTWARD
EXPRESSION, YOUR IMAGE, AND MANY
IMPORTANT PERSONALITY TRAITS. THE
MOON, ALTHOUGH MERELY THE EARTH'S
SATELLITE, IS ASTRONOMICALLY THE
SECOND MOST IMPORTANT BODY IN THE
SOLAR SYSTEM. FROM THE SIGN THAT IT
WAS IN AT YOUR BIRTH, IT INFLUENCES HOW
YOU REACT AND RESPOND TO SITUATIONS,
YOUR EMOTIONAL LEVEL AND, TO A CERTAIN
EXTENT, WHAT YOU HAVE INHERITED FROM
YOUR PARENTS AND ANCESTORS. HAVING
FOUND YOUR MOON SIGN IN THE SIMPLE
TABLES ON PAGES 56 TO 59, TURN TO THE
RELEVANT PAGES AND TAKE A STEP
FORWARD IN YOUR OWN SELF-KNOWLEDGE.

THE MOON IN
ARIES

YOUR ALERT AND CRITICAL VIRGOAN CHARACTERISTICS ARE SPICED
WITH VERY QUICK RESPONSES TO SITUATIONS. YOU ARE
EXCELLENT IN EMERGENCIES, BUT SHOULD ALWAYS BEWARE OF
TAKING PREMATURE, ILL-CONSIDERED ACTION.

Your Arien Moon adds many contrasting characteristics to your practically inclined Sun. You can react rapidly to most situations, and are good at grasping the immediate essentials of any set of circumstances.

Self-expression
You are always on the ball. There is, however, a drawback to this, since you may sometimes be impatient and too hasty. You will probably be far less cautious than many Sun sign Virgoans, and should always think twice before you commit yourself.

The greatest contrast between Aries and Virgo is an emotional one. You have powerful emotional resources, and will probably be able to express them freely and rewardingly.

Romance
You have a passionate side to your nature, and characteristic Virgoan modesty will be unlikely to inhibit your approach to sex. If you manage to follow your basic intuition and impulses, you should enjoy a truly rewarding love and sex life.

When you become involved in a relationship, you may find Virgo prompting you to have second thoughts. You may ask yourself if you are good enough for your partner. Try to ignore such doubts – they are the product of your Virgoan Sun, which will be trying to put a brake on the more forthright and passionate response of your Arien Moon.

Your well-being
Ariens often suffer from headaches, and Virgoans are prone to migraine. The cause will probably be a build-up of tension, to which you will be very prone. All Virgoans have a busy lifestyle that allows little time for relaxation, and your Arien Moon chimes in with this. You need to learn how to relax, and a discipline like

The Moon in Aries

yoga will help. It should, however, be noted that headaches are sometimes the result of slight kidney disorders.

You probably have a very fast metabolic rate, and will therefore be unlikely to put on excess weight.

Planning ahead

You may be far less careful with money than many people of your Sun sign. Try to control your Arien response to so-called bargains. If you are attracted to some big purchase, ask yourself if you really need it. This whole area is one that demands Virgoan caution.

Parenthood

The chances are that you will be less overtly critical of your children than many Virgoans, and this is no bad thing. If you get really involved in their hobbies, you will develop a marvellously positive rapport with them. You should have no problems with the generation gap.

THE MOON IN
TAURUS

YOUR SUN AND MOON SIGNS ARE BOTH OF THE EARTH ELEMENT,
AND YOU ARE THEREFORE A PRACTICAL PERSON. ALLOW
YOUR SLOW, CAREFUL RESPONSES TO SITUATIONS TO GUIDE YOU
WHEN DISTURBED BY VIRGOAN TENSION AND WORRY.

Both Virgo and Taurus are earth signs, and bestow practical common sense upon their subjects. Try, however, not to be over-cautious.

Self-expression
The elements of shyness or inhibition that can be a part of every Virgoan character could prompt you to develop a safe and predictable routine, which may allow little or no scope for adventure. Always aim to consider situations constructively, as challenges, taking each development step-by-step, with confident assurance. In this way you will make the most of your best qualities.

You have marvellous potential that needs to be positively expressed, perhaps through craftwork or music.

Romance
Your Taurean Moon gives you a tender and affectionate emotion that enhances your attitude to, and

expression of, love. If you allow it some freedom, an instinctive sensuality, which will no doubt delight your partner, should emerge.

The worst Taurean fault is possessiveness. Virgoans are extremely rational and logical, and it is this area of your personality that you should tune into if possessiveness becomes a problem. Remember also that you can be rather critical. If you avoid carping, and allow your love room to breathe, you will enjoy a rewarding relationship.

Your well-being
The Taurean body area is the throat, and yours could be vulnerable. Always keep a remedy at the ready, especially during the winter or if there is an influenza bug going around.

Your Virgoan metabolism may be somewhat slower than average, as Taureans tend to move slowly, consequently putting on weight quite

The Moon in Taurus

easily. You could also have a sneaking regard for chocolate and most rich foods. If you are at all worried or upset, a burst of "comfort eating" may need to be resisted.

Planning ahead

You have an excellent business sense, and should be able to make clever, canny investments. Taurus enjoys luxury and every creature comfort, and is very attracted to quality. On the whole, Virgo goes for economy and good value. Here, therefore, is a possible source of conflict that only you can resolve. Why not enjoy those quality luxuries, and feel no guilt?

Parenthood

You will work extremely hard in every way, but especially to give your children a good life. Make sure that you have time for fun and outings with them, and that you do not miss out on their company. You may tend to be strict and discipline them firmly. Do not overdo this, and try not to be too critical of their efforts.

THE MOON IN
GEMINI

BOTH VIRGO AND GEMINI ARE RULED BY THE PLANET MERCURY, SO
THERE IS GREAT EMPATHY BETWEEN THESE SIGNS.
YOU HAVE A SHARP MIND, BUT DO NOT LET GEMINIAN LOGIC BE
DAMAGED BY VIRGOAN CRITICISM AND NAGGING.

The planet Mercury rules over both Virgo and Gemini, and these two signs are of the mutable quality. You therefore like variety and change, and are extremely versatile.

Self-expression
Mercury is regarded as the planet of communication, so it is likely that you are an excellent communicator. You may be a good teacher, or perhaps you work in the media.

The worst Geminian faults are restlessness and superficiality. While you could have many tasks on the go at the same time, remember that you will get far more inner fulfilment if you complete everything you begin.

Romance
You may tend to fight shy of showing your true feelings. Once in love, however, your partner could well receive sackfuls of letters, postcards, poems, and the like from you. Try to

relax into your relationships, and be aware that while Virgoan modesty can be charming, it should not prevent you from enjoying a rich and rewarding sex life.

It is important for you to have a high level of friendship within any emotional relationship. Seek partners who are at least your intellectual equals, and who can challenge your extremely lively mind.

Your well-being
The Geminian body areas are the arms and hands: be extra careful when using tools, or when cooking. The body organ is the lungs, and it is therefore inadvisable for anyone with a Geminian influence to smoke.

You may be quite highly strung, since you have a great deal of nervous energy. This must be burned off through exercise that is both physically and mentally stimulating, for instance fast games such as

The Moon in Gemini

badminton, squash, or tennis. As a result of tension, you may suffer from migraine even more often than many Virgoans. Try to cultivate your sense of inner calm by learning some kind of relaxation technique.

Planning ahead
Mercury is the planet most closely associated with buying and selling. If you have something to sell, you will almost always contrive to get the best possible price for it. You may need to take professional advice when

investing, because there is a chance that your cautious, practical Virgoan Sun could sometimes fail you.

Parenthood
You will be a very lively parent, and will not find it difficult to keep well up with, or ahead of, your children's current crazes, ideas, and opinions.

You are, however, very critical, and may tend to deflate your children by being over-critical of their efforts. Be careful: such put-downs can, in the long run, be very damaging.

THE MOON IN
CANCER

VIRGO AND CANCER ARE THE TWO SIGNS OF THE ZODIAC MOST
PRONE TO WORRY. VIRGOAN WORRY IS INTELLECTUAL;
CANCERIAN, INTUITIVE AND IMAGINATIVE. YOU SHOULD AIM
TO BALANCE THESE TRAITS AGAINST EACH OTHER.

The Moon rules Cancer, and its influence over you is therefore very powerful, perhaps even to the point where you will show rather less than the average number of characteristics said to be typical of your Sun sign.

Self-expression

Your practical Virgoan Sun and extremely intuitive Moon suggest that you might possess a number of admirable virtues.

You have a very vivid and powerful imagination, which is probably highly spiced with creative potential. Try to express it whenever you can. For example, if you have a sneaking feeling that you would like to write, do not hesitate to do so.

Where your Sun and Moon signs meet all too well is in relation to anxiety. These signs seem to fight for first prize in the Zodiac where the tendency to worry is concerned. It will

work at two levels, and you can fight it in two ways. The Virgoan way is to analyze the details of a situation; the Cancerian way is to follow your instinct and intuition.

Romance

You no doubt possess a rather high emotional level, and are able to express it much more freely than many Virgoans. You also have the wonderful capacity to live a rich and fulfilling love and sex life, and the ability to contribute a great deal to a happy relationship. You must, however, recognize the fact that you can sometimes be too protective.

Your well-being

The Cancerian body area covers the chest and breasts. The sign has nothing to do with the disease of the same name, but women should, of course, check their breasts regularly. Because of your tendency to worry,

The Moon in Cancer

you may, at times, be subject to stomach (from Virgo) and digestive (from Cancer) problems. Aim for inner calm and peace, and avoid flapping about like a worried hen.

You may be an excellent cook, but should watch how much you eat. You could be more prone to weight gain than most Virgoans. If your metabolism is slow, try to speed it up a little, perhaps through exercise.

Planning ahead

You will be very careful, perhaps even over-cautious with money. However, you certainly have what it takes to

make money: a remarkably shrewd and intuitive business sense, which should enable you to invest wisely.

Parenthood

You make a marvellous, caring parent, and will want to "mother" your children. Try to accept the fact that they will eventually leave home and make their own lives. It is particularly important for women with this Sun and Moon combination to develop new interests at such times. Try not to be too sentimental, recalling "the old days" too relentlessly, otherwise the generation gap will loom large.

THE MOON IN
LEO

GIVE YOUR LEO MOON ROOM TO BREATHE. IT WILL PROVIDE
YOU WITH THE CONFIDENCE TO DO WHAT YOU WANT,
BECAUSE IT IS RIGHT FOR YOU. DO NOT LET SHYNESS CRAMP
YOUR STYLE OR INHIBIT YOU IN ANY WAY.

Your Leo Moon creates some very striking qualities that contrast strongly with those of your Virgoan Sun. Try to become more aware of them, and allow them to work for you.

Self-expression

You have greater self-confidence than many people of your Sun sign, and if you can combine this with the Virgoan ability to communicate your ideas, emotions, and opinions, you cannot fail to make excellent progress.

Should you be someone who initially seems to accept challenges and copes positively with situations, but then retreats on second thoughts, try to reach a better balance. Your Leo Moon is there to push you forward and boost your self-confidence.

In addition, in contrast to most Virgoans you have very good organizational ability. You do not need to be told everything that is expected of you, and you can cope

well in a crisis. You may have creative potential, and should try to fit time to express this into your busy schedule.

Romance

You have warm, fiery emotions and, because you are such a good communicator, should not find it difficult to express your feelings. You certainly have the capacity to love deeply and passionately, but must consciously dispel any typically Virgoan feelings of inferiority.

You will want to look up to your partners, and do everything possible to please them, but remember that relationships should be partnerships.

Your well-being

The Leo body area is said to cover the back and spine. These are therefore vulnerable, so make sure that you take enough exercise to keep them in really good condition. Many Virgoans love walking and jogging. If

40

The Moon in Leo

you feel that this applies to you, remember to make sure that you walk well, with a straight back.

The Leo body organ is the heart, and this organ, like all the others, needs regular exercise. You will probably be less prone to worry than most people of your Sun sign, and this characteristic is therefore less likely to affect your health.

Planning ahead

The contrast between Leo and Virgo will emerge in your attitude towards money. Your Moon sign instinct veers towards generosity, extravagance, and

quality. Your Virgoan Moon encourages a taste for simple things, of good value. Somewhere between the two is the point of balance.

You will probably invest soundly, provided your Leo Moon does not encourage you to put all your financial eggs in one basket.

Parenthood

Your natural enthusiasm will make you a lively parent. You will be less critical, and more encouraging, than most Virgoans. Take into account your children's opinions, and encourage lively debate among them.

THE MOON IN
VIRGO

BECAUSE BOTH THE SUN AND THE MOON WERE IN VIRGO ON THE
DAY OF YOUR BIRTH, YOU WERE BORN UNDER A NEW MOON.
SINCE VIRGO IS AN EARTH SIGN, THIS ELEMENT POWERFULLY
INFLUENCES YOUR PERSONALITY AND REACTIONS.

Should you study a list of your Sun
sign characteristics, you will
probably recognize that a great many
of them apply to you. On average, out
of a list of perhaps 20 traits of a Sun
sign listed in books or magazines,
most people will strongly identify
with 11 or 12. In your case, however,
the average increases considerably
because the Sun and Moon were both
in Virgo when you were born.

Self-expression

Your Sun sign will tend to make you
lively and talkative, but rather
cautious and, sometimes, perhaps
lacking in self-confidence; your Moon
sign causes you to react to challenges
in the same way.

You have an alert mind, and your
responses tend to be critical. Be
careful that you do not get too bogged
down in detail, and try consciously to
develop the ability to grasp the overall
concept of a suggestion or project.

Romance

Your Sun and Moon signs are not very
highly charged with emotion and,
when you are in love, you could well
be a little apprehensive about
expressing your feelings. Remember
that you are good with words, and do
not be afraid to say what you feel.
Take your time, however, since
nervousness can make you over-
talkative. Do not allow yourself to be
rushed into a relationship, but do not
make excuses, either, in order to avoid
committing yourself.

One area in which you should hold
back is in being critical of your
partners. Try and accept them for
what they are.

Your well-being

Everything that has been said about
health on pages 22 to 23 probably
applies directly to you. You are
possibly one of the Great Worriers of
the World, and this could affect your

The Moon in Virgo

digestion. You probably respond very well to most homeopathic and complementary medical treatments, in particular reflexology.

Your very high nervous energy can lead to a build-up of tension. Like many Virgoans, you may therefore benefit from yoga.

Planning ahead

You will not be very adventurous when it comes to money, and will spend carefully and wisely. Go for investments that show slow but steady growth. You may need professional guidance when you wish to invest or save some money.

Parenthood

You will stimulate your children's minds, but may be a little cool. They will benefit from sound explanations, but a cuddle is often more reassuring. Try not to be too critical. This will not be easy for you, although keeping up with your children's concerns will.

THE MOON IN
LIBRA

VIRGO IS ALL ACTION, WHILE LIBRA IS MORE RELAXED AND LAID BACK. IT IS IMPORTANT FOR YOU TO KEEP YOUR PHYSICAL AND INTELLECTUAL ENERGIES IN BALANCE. A LIBRAN MOON GIVES YOU A DIPLOMATIC STREAK THAT YOU MUST NOT SUPPRESS.

Your Libran Moon lightens your personality and helps you to take a rather more relaxed attitude to life than many Virgoans.

Self-expression

When confronted by problems, you may respond with "Que sera, sera" and, while for some Zodiac types this could prove a negative or complacent reaction, for you it is actually fitting, since it allows you a breathing space before your more energetic, tense nervous energy springs into action. One word of warning: you could be rather indecisive in certain situations, and, to counter the tendency, should bring your marvellously logical and critical Sun sign qualities into play.

Romance

You are very romantic at heart, and should not find it too difficult to relax into emotional and sexual relationships. In fact, your response to

people of the opposite sex is probably far more forthcoming than that of many Sun sign Virgoans.

Be careful that you do not rush into marriage or a permanent relationship, only to find that the man or woman of your choice is terribly irritating or does not come up to your standards.

You are probably more tactful and diplomatic towards your partners than most Virgoans. Shyness and modesty will be less dominant in you, and you should have no problem enjoying a rich and fulfilling love and sex life.

Your well-being

The Libran body organ is the kidneys. Virgoan headaches and migraines, which are due to stress and tension, may be exacerbated by your Libran Moon, since there is a possibility that slight kidney upsets could also give you headaches. However, your Moon sign should help to prevent too much tension from building up.

The Moon in Libra

You may have a slower metabolism than many Sun sign Virgoans, and could enjoy rather rich food. If you are at all prone to weight gain, try to adjust your diet, and do not allow yourself to get lazy about exercise.

Planning ahead

You may well be conscience-stricken when you have been extravagant. Try not to get too concerned about such things. You may not be terribly good at handling your finances, and should seek professional advice in this area,

especially if you want to buy shares or are considering an investment or some form of pension plan.

Parenthood

While you will be a fine parent, it is possible that your children may not always know precisely where they stand with you. Be careful, since this can cause problems. Aim to keep a balance. Remember, too, to keep abreast of your children's opinions and concerns, in order to avoid problems with the generation gap.

THE MOON IN
SCORPIO

YOU NEED TO GET TO THE BOTTOM OF ANY PROBLEM THAT YOU
ENCOUNTER, AND TO DELVE INTO IT IN GREAT DETAIL.
YOU HAVE MORE EMOTIONAL FORCE THAN MOST VIRGOANS, AND
SHOULD USE THIS POSITIVELY.

The earth element of a Virgoan Sun blends well with the water element of your Scorpio Moon, for in many respects these influences have certain qualities in common.

Self-expression

You will find research compelling, and should get involved in a subject into which you can delve in real depth.

You also have great determination and sense of purpose, and need to be emotionally involved with any work that you do. The inner psychological fulfilment that you will get out of this is essential to you, but you must learn to develop breadth of vision. While your flair for detail is marvellous, you may not always grasp overall concepts very well.

Romance

You need really rewarding sexual expression and fulfilment. This may not be simple, because you will be a demanding partner and, while capable of giving great sexual pleasure, you may well have special needs. Choose your partners with all the discrimination and care bestowed by your Virgoan Sun and Scorpio Moon.

The worst Scorpio fault is jealousy, and the worst Virgoan fault, that of being overly critical. Clearly, these can marry in a rather worrying way, so do consciously guard against them.

Your well-being

The Scorpio body area covers the genitals. Scorpio women should make sure they have regular check-ups, and men should regularly examine their testicles for irregularities. With your Sun and Moon combination, your throat may also be open to infections.

You may be very prone to Virgoan worry, as your Scorpio Moon gives you an active, fertile imagination that can sometimes prompt you to worry over nothing. This may lead to an upset

The Moon in Scorpio

stomach and minor ailments that are difficult to pin down. At such times, try to let Virgoan logic dominate.

Planning ahead
You are likely to have an instinctive business sense, and a natural ability to make money.

You probably also have considerably more expensive tastes than most other Virgoans, and will need to earn a good salary in order to allow for some costly indulgences.

Parenthood
You may be a far stricter parent than you realize, but in many ways this is not a bad thing at all. You are aiming to make your children grow up to be decent and considerate people. It may, however, be necessary for you to achieve a little more balance. Let yourself go, and allow yourself to express your enjoyment of life in your relationship with your children. In this way, you will have real fun and reduce generation gap problems.

THE MOON IN
SAGITTARIUS

DO NOT UNDERESTIMATE YOUR OWN INTELLIGENCE; YOU MAY
HAVE A GREAT CAPACITY FOR STUDY. BE CAREFUL
THAT YOUR SAGITTARIAN MOON DOES NOT GIVE OTHERS THE
IMPRESSION THAT YOU ARE UNCARING OR OFFHAND.

Both Virgo and Sagittarius bestow a good intellectual capacity, and make you adaptable to changing atmospheres and conditions. Your Sagittarian Moon makes you respond optimistically to challenges, and gives you a positive outlook. As a result, you should, in theory, be far less of a worrier than most Sun sign Virgoans.

Self-expression

You are always happy to become involved in the details of an argument but, because of your Sagittarian Moon, you have the breadth of vision and the ability to take in the overall situation as well. The worst Sagittarian fault happens to be restlessness; try to avoid it by developing consistency of effort.

There is an element of the "eternal student" about you. You can cope well with intellectual challenge, so it is quite important

that you always have an intellectually demanding project on hand. If your work constantly taxes your intellect, make sure that you spend some of your spare time involved in a physically demanding interest.

Romance

You have a fine, positive, fiery emotional force that will find its best expression in your love and sex life. You are unlikely to be shy or modest; your attitude to love is lively, and you have a great capacity to enjoy sexual relationships. You need partners who understand your need for an element of freedom and independence within a relationship. An even vaguely claustrophobic atmosphere will not suit you at all.

Your well-being

The Sagittarian body area covers the hips and thighs. Women who have this sign emphasized will tend to put

The Moon in Sagittarius

on weight in those areas. Only exercise and a very controlled, regular diet will help. The Sagittarian organ is the liver, and it is surprising how easy it is for you to feel "liverish". Your body and mind must be kept in good running order, like a well-oiled machine. If they are not, you will suffer far more than most people.

Planning ahead

You have something of a gambling spirit, and it could well need careful control. It is related to a sneaking love of taking risks. If you are attracted to get-rich-quick schemes, always make sure that you allow your more cautious Virgoan self to have its say before embarking on them.

Parenthood

Your children will appreciate your enthusiastic responses to their suggestions, and you will not find it difficult to stimulate their minds and keep them active. They are unlikely to turn into couch potatoes, slumped in front of the television set for hours on end. If you can control any overtly critical qualities that spring from your Virgoan Sun, you ought not to experience generation gap problems.

THE MOON IN
CAPRICORN

YOUR CAPRICORNIAN MOON WILL EITHER HELP YOU TO SCALE THE
HEIGHTS OR HOLD YOU BACK. PRAISE YOURSELF AS OFTEN AS
POSSIBLE AND YOU WILL GET TO THE TOP. FALL INTO INHIBITING
SELF-CRITICISM AND YOU WILL NOT.

You are a very practical, sensible, and dependable person. Your Capricornian Moon can work for you in one of two ways. You will either respond well to challenge, and be very ambitious to succeed, stepping with great agility over every difficulty that crosses your path, and eventually reaching the top; or you will respond very negatively, declining to accept responsibility on the grounds that you cannot cope, or do not have the brains, the stamina, or the self-confidence. It is even possible that you may recognize both of these tendencies in yourself.

Self-expression
If you are rather timid, ask yourself whether this is due to the influence of your Virgoan Sun. The blending of the influences of your Sun and Moon is, in many ways, a great help in countering this tendency, and provides sound building blocks for

your personality. You can develop a reputation for reliability and common sense, and your truly practical outlook on life is enviable.

Romance
Capricorn is a cool, unemotional sign, and so is Virgo. You may therefore be inclined not to show your feelings all that readily. You will take your love and sex life very seriously, and may need to learn to relax more into your relationship if you are to experience a rewarding partnership.

Your well-being
The Capricornian body area covers the knees and shins, so if you enjoy long country hikes or jogs, you should make sure that your knees are always well protected.

The skin, teeth, and bones are also Capricorn-ruled, so use good-quality, natural skin products, and do not miss out on regular dental check-ups.

The Moon in Capricorn

Planning ahead

Because you are practical and cautious, you will no doubt be extremely careful with money. You probably enjoy putting carefully calculated sums aside regularly in some safe investment, for instance a building society account.

You may also have a liking for quality, and will discreetly go for the best whenever you can. There is a chance, however, that you may not always enjoy the fruits of your labours. You should find time to relax with a few well-chosen friends, and forget about entertaining only those people that you feel obliged to.

Parenthood

You may need to modify your conventional outlook by seeking other people's opinions. Do not be too critical of your children. Always make time for them, and do not constantly present them with logical arguments if they are upset. Give them a cuddle instead. Listen to their opinions, and you will avoid the generation gap.

THE MOON IN
AQUARIUS

VIRGOANS ARE PRACTICAL, AND OFTEN CONVENTIONAL. WITH AN
AQUARIAN MOON YOU ARE LIKELY TO RESPOND WELL TO NEW,
INVENTIVE, AND ORIGINAL IDEAS. IF YOU HAPPEN TO BE INTERESTED
IN UNTRIED CONCEPTS, DO NOT DISMISS YOUR INTUITIONS.

Your Aquarian Moon and your Virgoan Sun give you an intriguing and perhaps even somewhat enigmatic personality.

Self-expression
You have a very independent streak, and will often react to situations and to the suggestions of other people in a very individual way. More than this, when it comes to helping other people, you are all kindness.

You have plenty of originality, and probably a great deal of creative, artistic flair. Make sure that you have time to express this fully, as it will give you a great deal of satisfaction.

While your Virgoan Sun makes you practical and conventional, your Aquarian Moon attracts you to less conventional things. Beware of responding a little unpredictably at times; while surprising other people is lively fun, unpredictability can sometimes be embarrassing.

Romance
Both Virgo and Aquarius are emotionally cool, and it may not be very easy for you to show your true feelings. However, your Aquarian Moon shines brightly for you, giving you a very romantic streak and making you a faithful lover once committed. It can also bestow a film-star glamour that is devastatingly attractive. However, like a magnet, you can distance yourself from what you attract, and may at times appear entirely out of reach. If you relax and allow your romantic side to take over, you will enjoy a very rewarding love and sex life.

Your well-being
The Aquarian body area covers the ankles. Be very careful, as they are vulnerable when you are exercising or involved in sport. The circulation is also Aquarius-ruled, so even if you enjoy bracing, cold weather, do keep

The Moon in Aquarius

very warm. Your whole well-being may otherwise suffer, and you could feel uncomfortably stiff and aching.

You are less inclined to irrational worry than many Virgoans, and the effect of worry on your health is not potentially as bad as it tends to be for other Sun sign Virgoans.

Planning ahead

You are attracted to glamorous and expensive things, especially for your home and wardrobe. These will certainly eat into your finances and, while you are as practical as the next Virgoan, you could consider taking professional financial advice.

Parenthood

Your Aquarian Moon gives you a modern outlook that your children will really appreciate. You may, however, consciously need to express a little more emotional warmth from time to time, although your empathy should be excellent.

THE MOON IN
PISCES

VIRGO AND PISCES ARE POLAR OR OPPOSITE ZODIAC SIGNS, SO YOU
WERE BORN UNDER A FULL MOON. RESTLESSNESS AND
INNER DISCONTENT COULD BOTHER YOU. BE RATIONAL, AND DO
NOT BE SWAYED BY NEGATIVE EMOTIONS.

Each of us has a strong tendency to express certain attributes of our polar or opposite sign (the sign that is across the Zodiac circle from our Sun Sign). For Virgoans, the polar sign is Pisces and, because the Sun was in that sign when you were born, the polarity is expressed in a very interesting way.

Self-expression

You will be very sensitive to other people's suggestions and actions, and could be more easily hurt than most Virgoans. The kindness of Virgo is powerfully emphasized in your personality; you instinctively know when help is needed, and will respond immediately.

Neither Virgo nor Pisces are basically very self-confident. You have great potential and, if there is something that you long to do or wish to study, you should give yourself the opportunity to do so. Try not to give up too quickly or easily, and develop your powers of concentration and persistence of effort.

Romance

You are among the more emotional of Virgoans, and this is good. Being practical, and not lacking in common sense, you are also able to respond to lovers in a tender, warm, and sensual way. You need to feel secure in emotional and sexual relationships; then you make a wonderful partner.

The worst Piscean fault is deceptiveness. Your Piscean Moon may also make you self-deceptive. If you remain level-headed, you will find a partner on whom you can rely.

Your well-being

The Piscean body area covers the feet, and you may have difficulty in obtaining comfortable shoes. Foot exercise sandals are very good for you, and far preferable to bare feet.

	1975	1976	1977	1978	1979	1980	1981	1982	1983	1984	1985	1986	1987
JAN	♌	♑	♉	♍	♒	♊	♏	♓	♌	♐	♉	♍	♑
FEB	♎	♒	♋	♏	♈	♌	♐	♉	♍	♒	♊	♎	♓
MAR	♎	♓	♋	♏	♈	♍	♑	♉	♎	♒	♊	♏	♓
APR	♐	♈	♍	♑	♊	♎	♒	♋	♏	♈	♌	♑	♉
MAY	♑	♉	♎	♒	♋	♏	♓	♌	♐	♉	♍	♒	♊
JUN	♓	♋	♐	♈	♌	♑	♉	♎	♒	♊	♏	♓	♌
JUL	♈	♌	♑	♉	♍	♒	♋	♏	♓	♐	♐	♉	♍
AUG	♉	♎	♓	♋	♏	♈	♌	♐	♈	♎	♒	♊	♎
SEP	♋	♐	♈	♌	♐	♊	♎	♒	♊	♏	♓	♌	♐
OCT	♌	♑	♉	♍	♒	♋	♏	♓	♋	♐	♉	♍	♑
NOV	♎	♓	♋	♏	♓	♌	♎	♐	♉	♍	♒	♊	♓
DEC	♏	♈	♌	♐	♉	♍	♑	♊	♎	♓	♋	♐	♈

	1988	1989	1990	1991	1992	1993	1994	1995	1996	1997	1998	1999	2000
JAN	♊	♎	♒	♋	♏	♈	♌	♑	♉	♎	♒	♊	♏
FEB	♋	♐	♈	♍	♑	♉	♎	♒	♋	♏	♈	♌	♐
MAR	♌	♐	♉	♍	♒	♊	♎	♓	♋	♏	♈	♌	♑
APR	♍	♒	♊	♏	♓	♋	♐	♈	♍	♑	♊	♎	♓
MAY	♏	♓	♌	♐	♈	♍	♑	♉	♎	♒	♋	♏	♈
JUN	♐	♉	♍	♑	♊	♎	♓	♋	♐	♈	♌	♑	♉
JUL	♑	♊	♎	♒	♋	♐	♈	♌	♑	♉	♎	♒	♋
AUG	♓	♌	♐	♈	♍	♑	♉	♎	♓	♋	♏	♓	♌
SEP	♉	♍	♑	♊	♏	♓	♋	♏	♈	♌	♑	♉	♎
OCT	♊	♎	♒	♋	♐	♈	♌	♑	♉	♎	♒	♊	♏
NOV	♌	♐	♈	♍	♑	♉	♎	♒	♋	♏	♈	♌	♑
DEC	♍	♑	♉	♎	♒	♋	♏	♈	♌	♐	♉	♍	♒

THE SOLAR SYSTEM

THE STARS, OTHER THAN THE SUN, PLAY NO PART IN THE SCIENCE
OF ASTROLOGY. ASTROLOGERS USE ONLY THE BODIES IN THE
SOLAR SYSTEM, EXCLUDING THE EARTH, TO CALCULATE HOW OUR
LIVES AND PERSONALITIES CHANGE.

Pluto
Pluto takes 246 years to travel around
the Sun. It affects our unconscious
instincts and urges, gives us strength
in difficulty, and perhaps emphasizes
any inherent cruel streak.

Neptune
Neptune stays in each sign for 14
years. At best it makes us sensitive
and imaginative; at worst it
encourages deceit and carelessness,
making us worry.

Uranus
Uranus's influence can make us
friendly, kind, eccentric, inventive,
and unpredictable.

Saturn
In ancient times, Saturn was the most
distant known planet. Its influence
can limit our ambition and make us
either overly cautious (but practical),
or reliable and self-disciplined.

PLUTO

NEPTUNE

URANUS

SATURN

Jupiter

Jupiter encourages expansion, optimism, generosity, and breadth of vision. It can, however, also make us wasteful, extravagant, and conceited.

Mars

Much associated with energy, anger, violence, selfishness, and a strong sex drive, Mars also encourages decisiveness and leadership.

JUPITER

The Moon

Although it is a satelite of the Earth, the Moon is known in astrology as a planet. It lies about 240,000 miles from the Earth and, astrologically, is second in importance to the Sun.

MERCURY

THE MOON VENUS

 EARTH

MARS

The Sun

The Sun, the only star used by astrologers, influences the way we present ourselves to the world – our image or personality; the "us" we show to other people.

Venus

The planet of love and partnership, Venus can emphasize all our best personal qualities. It may also encourage us to be lazy, impractical, and too dependent on other people.

Earth

Every planet contributes to the environment of the Solar System, and a person born on Venus would no doubt be influenced by our own planet in some way.

Mercury

The planet closest to the Sun affects our intellect. It can make us inquisitive, versatile, argumentative, perceptive, and clever, but maybe also inconsistent, cynical, and sarcastic.